W9-ALM-019

GREEN IDEAS

Anita Yasuda

j333.72
YAS

www.av2books.com

AV² by Weigl brings you media enhanced books that support active learning.

AV² provides enriched content that supplements and complements this book. Weigl's AV² books strive to create inspired learning and engage young minds for a total learning experience.

Go to **www.av2books.com**, and enter this book's unique code. You will have access to video, audio, web links, quizzes, a slide show, and activities.

BOOK CODE

U810201

Audio
Listen to sections of the book read aloud.

Video
Watch informative video clips

Web Link
Find research sites and play interactive games.

Try This!
Complete activities and hands-on experiments.

Due to the dynamic nature of the Internet, some of the URLs and activities provided as part of AV² by Weigl may have changed or ceased to exist. AV² by Weigl accepts no responsibility for any such changes. All media enhanced books are regularly monitored to update addresses and sites in a timely manner. Contact AV² by Weigl at 1-866-649-3445 or av2books@weigl.com with any questions, comments, or feedback.

Published by AV² by Weigl
350 5th Avenue, 59th Floor
New York, NY 10118
Website: www.av2books.com   www.weigl.com

Copyright ©2011 AV² by Weigl
All rights reserved. No part of this publication may be reproduced, stored in a retrieval system, or transmitted in any form or by any means, electronic, mechanical, photocopying, recording, or otherwise, without the prior written permission of the publisher.

Library of Congress Cataloging-in-Publication Data available upon request.
Fax 1-866-44-WEIGL for the attention of the Publishing Records department.

ISBN 978-1-61690-094-6 (hard cover)
ISBN 978-1-61690-095-3 (soft cover)

Printed in the United States of America in North Mankato, Minnesota
1 2 3 4 5 6 7 8 9 0   14 13 12 11 10

062010
WEP264000

Project Coordinators: Heather C. Hudak, Robert Famighetti
Design: Terry Paulhus
Project Editor: Emily Dolbear
Photo Research: Edward A. Thomas
Layout and Production: Tammy West

Every reasonable effort has been made to trace ownership and to obtain permission to reprint copyright material. The publishers would be pleased to have any errors or omissions brought to their attention so that they may be corrected in subsequent printings.

Weigl acknowledges Getty Images as its primary image supplier for this title.

CONTENTS

MAKING THE WORLD A GREENER PLACE

How can you make the world a greener place? You can help the planet by reducing your **carbon footprint**. A carbon footprint is the measure of **greenhouse gases** produced by human activities.

Greenhouse gases are produced by burning **fossil fuels**. People burn fossil fuels for electricity, heating, and powering vehicles. One of the biggest causes of **climate change** is the greenhouse gas known as carbon dioxide. Many scientists believe that carbon **emissions** are more damaging to Earth than any other kind of pollution.

There are many ways you can reduce your carbon footprint. One way is to walk or ride your bike instead of riding in a car. You can turn off lights when you leave a room to reduce energy waste. Reusing plastic shopping bags to carry other items is another way to help the environment. You can recycle newspaper so that fewer trees are chopped down to make new paper.

WHAT ARE GREEN IDEAS?

Green ideas are original and eco-friendly solutions to environmental problems that face our planet. Some of these creative ideas are high-tech. They involve industry and manufacturing. To make these green ideas work, new laws must be passed, and countries throughout the world must cooperate. Other green ideas are low-tech. These ideas can be put into action by individuals. People can make the planet a greener place by recycling, reusing, reducing waste, and taking part in celebrations that spread the message about protecting Earth. Green ideas encourage people to take action. Think about some different objects that you use every day. What resources were used to make these objects? What happened to the packages that once contained them? If the object is a replacement, what happened to the old one? How can you reduce, reuse, and recycle in your everyday life?

1 GOING GREEN ONLINE

Green ideas can be used and shared on the World Wide Web. Websites, blogs, and online newsletters provide a virtual community for those interested in living green. People are not limited by geography. They can get ideas from all over the world. They can participate in green discussions often and whenever it is convenient. People can even find ways to save energy while using the Internet.

WAYS GREEN IDEAS ARE BEING USED AND SHARED OVER THE INTERNET

Use Green Web Hosts Energy is used every time people go online. As Internet demand grows, so does its energy use. Scientists believe that Internet energy use rises 10 percent every year. Web hosts are looking for ways to lower their use. In the United States, green Web hosts use **renewable** energy sources, such as the Sun, wind, or water. Their offices may use eco-friendly design and energy-efficient LED lighting. The letters LED stand for light-emitting diode. Some Web hosts plant trees to offset their carbon footprint.

Save Energy On average, the energy consumed in one second of browsing the Web creates .001 ounces (20 milligrams) of carbon dioxide. If you have a computer, check the settings and make sure it automatically goes into "sleep," standby, or hibernate mode when it is idle for a few minutes. A computer uses far less electricity in these modes. To save even more energy, turn off computers, monitors, and printers at the end of the day or whenever they are not in use for a long period of time.

Share Information Blogs and websites spread green ideas over the Web. Some sites are run by government organizations such as the U.S. Environmental Protection Agency (EPA). The EPA website has green information for homes and businesses, as well as a carbon calculator that shows people their carbon footprint. Other sites are run by individuals. If you are interested in learning

more about how to do almost anything green, there are online sources that can help. Can you find any online sources to help you make the world a greener place? Ask an adult to help you find suitable sites.

"We can create a more **sustainable**, cleaner and safer world by making wiser energy choices."
–Robert Alan, writer and activist

2 LEARNING ABOUT "PRECYCLING"

"Precycling" is a green idea that helps stop waste before it happens. People who precycle consider the options before they buy an item and give priority to items that have green packaging. By making better decisions, people can create less waste, fewer **recyclables**, and use less energy.

WAYS TO PRECYCLE

Think Twice

There is enough trash thrown away each day in the United States to fill 63,000 garbage trucks. If people thought more about every purchase, that number could be much lower. Precycling invites

people to borrow, rent, or buy used products. Making green choices is not hard, but sometimes it takes a little homework. What green choices could you make to help reduce waste at your home or school?

"The packaging for a microwavable 'microwave' dinner is programmed for a shelf life of maybe six months, a cook time of two minutes and a **landfill** dead-time of centuries."
–David Wann, writer and activist

Shop Green Green grocery shopping can reduce the amount of waste your family produces. Instead of buying items with a great deal of packaging, buy items loose. Many healthful foods, such as fresh fruits and vegetables, tend to have less packaging. Buying items in bulk and sharing with family or friends can cut down on waste. Remember to take canvas or other types of reusable bags with you every time you shop. Many grocery stores even give discounts to customers who bring their own bags.

Reuse Americans throw out enough paper and plastic cutlery every year to circle Earth 300 times. One important precycling idea is to avoid buying items that can be used only once. Try to choose items that can be used many times. Instead of disposable plastic bags for sandwiches, try using containers that can be refilled. Throwing away paper creates a great deal of waste. How could such packaging be used again?

3 USING RECYCLING
ROBOTS

Recycling is an important green idea. It saves natural resources and energy, and it reduces emissions of greenhouse gases that add to **global warming**. Even after learning these facts, people are still throwing away items that could be recycled. One green idea is to use robots that make it easier for people to recycle.

WAYS ROBOTS ARE BEING USED TO HELP IN WASTE MANAGEMENT

Helping People

In recent years, robots have been used as a green alternative to traditional waste disposal. The Dustbot robot in Italy is the first robot in the world to remove trash from people's homes. Unlike garbage trucks, which usually run on fossil fuels, the Dustbot is electric and produces no pollution. Due to its small size, designers hope the robot will be especially useful in densely populated areas where it can be difficult for garbage trucks to travel. People give the robot an address where it is needed by calling it on their cell phones. The robot has a screen that displays four waste groups. They are

plastic, glass, organic, and other waste. Once a person selects the group the waste belongs to, a large drawer opens on the robot, and the waste is placed inside.

Testing Ideas

Green ideas make it easier for people to recycle. A robot built in Japan helps people tell the difference between recyclable and non-recyclable plastic. The robot uses lasers to sort six different types of plastic. Right now, the robot is only being used for testing. It is too large and expensive for home use. It is hoped that, in the future, smaller versions will be available to the public.

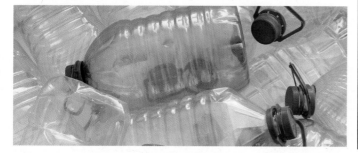

> "I am optimistic that this generation will have the foresight and the will to begin the task of forging a sustainable society."
>
> *–Gaylord Nelson, U.S. senator and founder of Earth Day*

Teaching Tools

Robots can teach people to be green. The Recycling and Environment Robot, created in Japan, first squeezes an object in its "hand." It then determines the kind of material the object is made from, and places it in the appropriate recycling bin. The robot also has a speech program. This allows it to answer questions about recycling. Simpler talking robots are also used to encourage people to dispose of waste. For example, Percy Penguin trash bins can be seen in Great Britain. The bins are placed in schools, hospitals, and other public places where many children can be found. Percy congratulates anyone who "feeds" litter to him.

FINDING NEW USES FOR
ELECTRONICS

An item you no longer need may be the very item someone else wants. Giving away an unwanted item creates bonds within communities and is good for the environment. The energy used in making something new and disposing of the old item is saved. The choice to repair an item can even create work for an individual. Reusing electronics, such as old computers and cell phones, is a green idea.

WAYS REUSING ELECTRONICS CAN HELP THE ENVIRONMENT

Reduce E-waste

E-waste, or electronic garbage, is one of the fastest-growing sources of pollution. Worldwide, 40 million tonnes (36 million metric tons) of e-waste are generated every year. These materials are often thrown away incorrectly. The chemicals they contain can leak out, harming people and the environment. Collecting, reusing, and recycling e-waste are green ideas. Alex Lin, a student in Rhode Island, put together a team that collects e-waste. Old computers are fixed up and donated to families that cannot afford to buy a computers. Can you think of ways to collect and reuse e-waste in your community?

"Extending the life of a computer is the most effective way to reduce its overall impact."
–Eric Williams, *editor*, Computers and the Environment

Share Goods

Giving away unwanted electronic goods to charity is a green idea. It keeps e-waste out of landfills. Many national and local charities take unwanted computers. These are then upgraded and used in schools or given to people who need them. The global nonprofit group Freecycle aims to keep objects out of landfills. This group asks its members to give and get "free stuff" in their towns instead of throwing items away. The organization has more than seven million members around the world.

Save Raw Materials

Green ideas make use of existing resources. Electronics, such as computers and cell phones, contain up to 60 different **elements**. Some of these electronics contain metals such as silver and gold, which can be **reclaimed** and then reused. Other elements, such as lead and mercury, are toxic. These need to be kept out of landfills. Cell phones should never be thrown away. They can be donated or recycled. According to Nokia, a cell phone company, if all their users recycled just one phone, more than 80,000 tons (73,000 tonnes) of raw materials would be saved.

5 PEOPLE WORKING TOGETHER

Some green ideas bring everyone in a community together. One person can make a difference, but a group of people can be even more effective. Local events, newsletters, and websites are an important part of advertising green projects. Over time, these green ideas will have a lasting effect in the community.

WAYS GREEN IDEAS CAN INVOLVE A COMMUNITY

Create a Project

Community programs require teamwork. Most successful green ideas involve a group of people working together. Once a team is formed, a group can think of ways to help create a greener community. The ideas should be simple to encourage more people to take action. The team could focus on energy, waste, water, or food. Green ideas involve healthful living.

Do you live in an area where more children could walk or ride bikes to school? Is there a local farmers' market in your community? If not, how could the community come together to create one?

"Planting a tree has universal power in every culture and every society on Earth, and it is a way for individual men, women and children to participate in creating solutions for the environmental crisis."
—*Al Gore, environmental activist and former U.S. vice president*

Take Part in the United Nations Billion Tree Campaign

Trees take in carbon dioxide, which they use to make food. They also release oxygen into the air. Cutting down trees in large numbers contributes to increasing the amount of carbon dioxide in the air. This leads to global warming. A green idea to fight global warming is the United Nations Billion Tree Campaign. The campaign helps communities plant trees. The hope is that a billion trees will be planted around the world each year. You can find out more about how the program works and how you might help by visiting **www.unep.org/billiontreecampaign**.

Advertise the Project

Creating a catchy **slogan**, such as "Eat Local" or "Zero Footprint," that quickly sums up the focus of a project is a good way to get attention for the project. Green slogans get people thinking and talking about change. Design your own slogan. How would it encourage people to go green?

6 LEARNING ABOUT BOLD GREEN IDEAS

Some green ideas are so bold that they make people look at the world from a new point of view. By challenging us, these green ideas stir debate. They make people question how they live now and how they could live in the future.

WAYS GREEN IDEAS MAY BE USED IN THE FUTURE

Use Flying Bikes
Many U.S. cities and towns have bike lanes on their roads. Bulgarian designer Martin Angelo has imagined lanes that will eventually be high above the streets. In 2009, he designed a "flying" bicycle lane. This bold green idea won the 2009 International Line of Site competition. Inspired by ski lifts, he imagined a system of cables with two parallel wires attached to a bike. One wire is for the wheels, and one is for the handlebars. Unlike a ski lift, the flying bike lane does not use electricity. Cyclists pedal to move their bikes. The system can be set up almost anywhere, including areas too crowded for traditional bike lanes.

Ride On Demand
Most large cities have a bus system that runs on a schedule. The buses run whether they have people on them or not. On-demand buses are a green idea to lower transportation costs and buses' effect on the environment. On-demand buses are being tested in a few cities in Japan. To use the buses, passengers arrange a pickup and drop-off along the bus route. People can book their stops online or at bus stations. A bus route is then determined based on advance bookings.

> "We shall require a substantially new manner of thinking if mankind is to survive."
>
> –Albert Einstein, physicist and philosopher

Learn About Masdar
A "carbon-neutral" city is one that does not produce carbon dioxide emissions. Masdar, in Abu Dhabi, United Arab Emirates, will be the first carbon-neutral city. Located in a hot, dry region that gets plenty of sunshine, Masdar will be powered by solar and other renewable energy sources. The city will attempt to reduce its waste to zero. Biological waste will be converted to fertilizer or fuel, and all other waste will be recycled or reused. It is expected that 50,000 people will live there. Cars will not be allowed to enter.

7 MAKING WORK GREENER

For years, going to work meant getting in a car, riding a bus, or taking a train. Today, thanks to computers, many people can work from their homes. Eliminating a worker's daily **commute** is both environmentally friendly and efficient. It cuts down on energy use and saves resources. Allowing employees to work from home, or telecommute, is one of the most important ways an office can go green.

WAYS COMMUNICATION TECHNOLOGY MAKES WORK GREENER

Telecommute
The greenest commutes produce little or no pollution. In many areas of the United States, public transportation is not an option. Just about every employee must use a car to get to work. This uses large amounts of fuel and creates pollution. Working from home helps people reduce their carbon footprint. Transportation costs and the effect on the environment are reduced. Office energy needs are lowered. Even federal and state governments are taking part in this green idea. In Utah, 20 to 25 percent of the state's employees work from home two days a week.

Teleconference
Some companies use teleconferencing to allow employees in different locations to attend a meeting without traveling to the meeting site. Teleconferencing uses web cameras and other telecommunication technology to link people online. Presentations and meetings can involve employees all over the world. Teleconferencing is not only easy and cheap, but green as well. After the initial cost of buying equipment, virtual meetings save money for companies. They also save resources.

"Eco-smart bosses and workers everywhere are giving this carbon-footprint-shrinking solution a go."
–*Megan Cohen, writer*

Webcast
A webcast is a file used by businesses to distribute, or stream, information over the Web. A webcast can be used to present information to people in any part of the world, so that people do not need to travel to an event or a meeting. For example, webcast technology can be used by a company to announce a new product to customers, journalists, and other interested people who are located in many places. Webcasting is positive for the environment. It lowers the carbon footprint of the company and its clients. How might webcasting be used at your school?

USING GREEN DESIGN

8

"People power" is kinetic energy. It is the energy of motion. Someday soon, people power may be used as a green energy source like sunlight and wind. When people move, energy is produced. Much of this energy is lost. Some exciting green designs take energy from people and change it into electricity. It is then used to run machines.

WAYS TO TURN FOOTSTEPS INTO RENEWABLE ENERGY

Push a Revolving Door

Every green building may collect energy from people one day. This energy could be converted to electricity. The design firm Fluxxlab has created a revolving door that can collect energy from people. Every time a person pushes on the door, energy is produced. The door changes this energy into electricity. Enough is produced to power 16 light bulbs for one day. A coffee shop in the Netherlands called Natuurcafé La Porte uses a similar system to produce 4,600 kilowatt-hours of energy a year. An LED display on the door shows the amount of energy created when a person walks through.

Walk on Energy-Generating Floors

Some subway stations in Japan use energy-saving floors. When the Tokyo subway system needed to be updated in 2008, the system's operators decided to emphasize renewable energy. New station floors actually produce energy. The floors are fitted with power-generating mats that take the energy

created by pedestrian footsteps and convert it into electricity. The power is then used to run ticket gates and display systems in the station.

Create People Power

Green ideas consider how to make the most of resources. Sainsbury's, a British supermarket chain, opened its first "people powered" store in 2009. The company put kinetic road plates in the store's parking lot. When a car drives over the plates, it produces a vibration. The kinetic energy of the vibration is then converted to electricity. This electricity powers the equipment at the store's checkout counters. Sainsbury's system is helping the store reduce its carbon footprint.

"I don't accept the conventional wisdom that suggests that the American people are unable or unwilling to participate in a national effort to transform the way we use energy. I think the American people are ready to be part of a mission. I believe that."

–Barack Obama, *president of the United States*

GREEN IDEAS FOR
CLEAN AIR

9

Some gases and other substances in the air can be harmful to people, plants, and animals. They can also harm the environment in other ways. These substances are described as air pollution. Air pollution can make people and animals sick and can harm crops and other plants. Too much of the gas carbon dioxide in the air can contribute to global warming. Scientists are using green ideas to make the air we breathe cleaner.

WAYS TO REDUCE AIR POLLUTION THROUGH NEW TECHNOLOGY

Learn About "Trees"
Green ideas make use of cutting-edge technology. Klaus Lackner, a scientist at Columbia University, designed a **synthetic** tree. It collects carbon 1,000 times faster than a real tree. The synthetic tree absorbs carbon dioxide through its "leaves." The leaves are made from a plastic material. Once the carbon dioxide is absorbed, it is compressed and stored as a liquid. Lackner believes that synthetic trees could help reduce the buildup of carbon dioxide in the atmosphere. One tree can absorb the carbon dioxide produced by 20 cars. Synthetic trees cost about $30,000 to build. In the future, if synthetic trees become cheaper to use, where do you think they should be placed?

Investigate Ideas
In France, scientists have developed concrete that can break down pollutants. The concrete is treated with **photocatalysts**. These use solar energy to speed up chemical reactions. When the concrete comes in contact with light, the photocatalysts break down pollutants that collect on the surface of the concrete. This prevents the pollutants from being released into the air. Buildings made from this concrete are basically self-cleaning. In what places could this concrete be put to good use?

Know the Clean Air Act
Green laws protect people and the environment. One example of a green federal law in the United States is the Clean Air Act. Passed by Congress in 1970, the law gave the Environmental Protection Agency (EPA) the power to, among other things, protect air quality. The act stated that it was the EPA's job to try to prevent further air pollution by regulating such things as motor vehicle emissions.

"The 1970 Clean Air Act amendments . . . paved the way for the widespread consensus in our country today that air pollution control must be a top priority of the federal government."
—*Paul G. Rogers, former chair of the House Subcommittee on Health and the Environment*

10 CELEBRATING EARTH

Celebrating the natural wonders of Earth is one way to get people thinking about the importance of living green. All over the world, there are special events where green ideas are shared. These events can raise environmental awareness.

WAYS TO CELEBRATE THE EARTH

Take a Stand

It takes only one person to make a difference. Gaylord Nelson, who was a U.S. senator from Wisconsin, knew this. He worked for many years to have environmental laws passed. He felt people needed to do more to protect natural resources. To get all Americans involved, Nelson thought there should be a day when people could focus on protecting the planet. A group of people, made up mostly of college students, helped spread the word. On April 22, 1970, the first Earth Day was held.

Learn About Earth Hour

The first Earth Hour was held in Sydney, Australia, in 2007. More than two million homes and businesses turned out their lights for one hour. Today, countries all over the world hold Earth Hour events. In 2010, more than 120 countries participated. At large monuments, such as the Eiffel Tower in Paris and the Colosseum in Rome, lights were switched off to bring attention to the importance of reducing energy consumption.

In daily life, a simple action, such as turning off lights when they are not needed, can lower our carbon footprint.

Take Part in Earth Day

Green ideas are meant to be shared. An idea will have a bigger impact when more people know about it and are able to act upon it. The Earth Day idea started with just one person, but more than 20 million Americans took part in the first Earth Day celebration. This event helped put pressure on the U.S. government to make environmental protection a priority. Earth Day is now an annual event on April 22, and there are Earth Day organizations worldwide. What Earth Day activities does your school and community plan? What can you do to raise awareness about Earth Day at your school?

"The purpose of Earth Day was to get a nationwide demonstration of concern for the environment so large that it would shake the political establishment."
—*Gaylord Nelson, founder of Earth Day*

10 Greenest Cities in the World

1 Reykjavik, Iceland
This green city is known for its clean energy sources. By 2050, the city plans to be free of any dependence on fossil fuels.

2 Portland, Oregon
Portland's light rail system, numerous bike lanes, and open spaces make it one of the greenest cities in the United States.

3 Curitiba, Brazil
This city has one of the best public transit systems in the world. A recycling program aimed at children rewards recyclables with school supplies, toys, and tickets to shows.

ARCTIC OCEAN

NORTH AMERICA

PACIFIC OCEAN

ATLANTIC OCEAN

SOUTH AMERICA

N
W   E
S

Scale: 621 Miles
0   1,000 Kilometers

SOUTHERN OCEAN

4 Malmö, Sweden
Parks and eco-friendly neighborhoods make this city a green model.

5 Vancouver, Canada
This green city is a leader in hydroelectric power and has a 100-year plan for sustainability.

The top green cities in the world use clean and renewable energy. People are able to walk or ride bikes instead of relying on cars. Green cities plant trees and create more green spaces to reduce carbon footprints.

San Francisco, California
Almost half of San Francisco's residents walk, bike, or take public transportation to work every day. Among many other green initiatives, the city has banned non-recyclable plastic bags.

Bahía de Caráquez, Ecuador
Programs to **compost** organic waste from public markets and control **erosion** make this city a favorite for eco-tourists.

Copenhagen, Denmark
A long-term green plan, clean waterways, and public transit won this green city the European Environmental Management Award.

Sydney, Australia
This green city was the first to hold an Earth Hour, in which electric lights were turned off for one hour to raise environmental awareness.

London, England
London's Climate Change Action plan, introduced in 2007, laid out a plan to drastically reduce the city's carbon dioxide emissions by 2027.

Green Careers

Green technology is used by many industries, from manufacturing to engineering. Here are two green career options in the technological field.

Environmental Engineer

Career

With the growing number of environmental projects, environmental engineers are in demand all over the world. Some work as consultants. A consultant will have different clients, which may include private companies and governments. The engineer is hired to create a green solution for a particular situation faced by each client. Green engineers may look for ways to reduce the effects of global warming. They collect data, study the results, and find a solution.

Education

To become an engineer, you must have a college degree, usually with a major in engineering, biology, or chemistry. Some environmental engineers attend graduate school for an advanced degree in environmental studies.

Environmental Scientist

Career

Environmental scientists must find ways for dealing with the effect people have on the environment. A scientist may conduct studies on pollution in the air, water, or soil, and on ways to reduce such pollution. An environmental scientist may work in a lab, an office, or on location. Scientists must learn new technology. They attend conferences and other meetings. They also read about the results of other people's research to learn about the latest advances in their field. They may be employed by a government agency, nonprofit organization, or university. Some may work for a private company, while others have their own consulting businesses.

Education

A college degree in a science field, such as chemistry, biology, or Earth sciences, is required. Many scientists have graduate degrees.

What have you learned about Being Green?

What have you learned about green ideas?
Take this quiz to test your knowledge.

1 How much carbon dioxide is produced by one second of Web browsing?

2 What is e-waste?

3 What does "precycling" mean?

4 Which city held the first Earth Hour?

5 What is the name of the U.S. government agency in charge of protecting the environment in the United States?

6 How can you lower your computer's energy usage?

7 When was the first Earth Day held?

8 What are some of the benefits of recycling electronics?

ANSWERS: 1. .001 ounces (20 milligrams) **2.** Electronic garbage, or discarded electronics **3.** Stopping waste before it happens **4.** Sydney, Australia **5.** Environmental Protection Agency, or EPA **6.** Have the computer hibernate when idle; turn it off when not in use **7.** April 22, 1970 **8.** Saving raw materials and keeping toxic materials out of landfills

Time to Debate

ISSUE Should all schools be required to have recycling programs?

Schools can play an important role in reducing waste. Setting up a recycling program is one way schools can go green. Aluminum cans, cardboard, printer cartridges, and paper are all commonly used school materials. Many of these materials can be recycled. Making recycling easier is a green idea that helps a new recycling program succeed. Many communities offer help to schools that want to begin a recycling program. San Jose, California, has a San Jose Go Green Schools Program. The city provides free assistance to schools, including maintenance and technical support. According to the city, San Jose schools dispose of more than 3,700 tons (3,360 tonnes) of paper each year. If schools recycle 1 ton (0.9 tonnes) of paper, this would be the equivalent of saving 4,110 kilowatts of energy.

PROS

1. Recycling teaches kids green habits for adulthood, which is good for the planet's future.
2. There may be an opportunity for a school to earn money by recycling certain items, such as printer cartridges or bottles.
3. Recycling conserves natural resources, saves energy in the manufacturing of new products, and reduces the need for landfills.

CONS

1. Setting up a paper collection program can be expensive.
2. Separating metals, plastic, and paper from other garbage takes time.
3. It sometimes can be difficult to tell whether particular items are recyclable or not.

WORDS TO KNOW

carbon footprint: an estimate of how much carbon dioxide is put into the atmosphere by the activities of a person or a company or the activities at a place

climate change: human-generated changes to the world environment; droughts, forest fires, and severe storms are just a few of the ways this can affect the United States

commute: to travel to and from a person's workplace

compost: organic material derived from such things as kitchen and yard waste that is used by gardeners or farmers to enrich the soil

elements: substances that contain only one kind of atom

emissions: substances discharged into the air

erosion: a natural process by which rocks and soil are broken loose from Earth's surface

e-waste: electronic garbage, in the form of obsolete or discarded electronics

fossil fuels: natural resources, such as coal, oil, and natural gas; all fossil fuels contain carbon and come from the remains of living things

global warming: an increase in Earth's average atmospheric temperature that may be caused by the greenhouse effect

greenhouse gases: carbon dioxide and other gases in the atmosphere that can contribute to global warming

landfill: a place where waste material is deposited

photocatalysts: substances that bring about a chemical reaction when exposed to light

reclaimed: obtained from a waste product and made usable again

recyclables: items capable of being used again

renewable: referring to resources that will always be available if used wisely, such as solar energy or lumber

slogan: a distinctive phrase or motto used by a group, manufacturer, or person

sustainable: capable of being continued without greatly harming the environment

synthetic: produced artificially

INDEX

Log on to www.av2books.com

AV² by Weigl brings you media enhanced books that support active learning. Go to **www.av2books.com**, and enter the special code inside the front cover of this book. You will gain access to enriched and enhanced content that supplements and complements this book. Content includes video, audio, web links, quizzes, a slide show, and activities.

Audio
Listen to sections of the book read aloud.

Video
Watch informative video clips.

Web Link
Find research sites and play interactive games.

Try This!
Complete activities and hands-on experiments.

WHAT'S ONLINE?

Try This! Complete activities and hands-on experiments.	 **Web Link** Find research sites and play interactive games.	**Video** Watch informative video clips.	**EXTRA FEATURES**
Pages 12-13 Try this activity about reusing electronics.	**Pages 8-9** Link to more information about precycling.	**Pages 4-5** Watch a video about green ideas.	**Audio** Hear introductory audio at the top of every page.
Pages 16-17 Complete an activity about green ideas of the future.	**Pages 10-11** Learn more about waste management.	**Pages 14-15** Learn more about communities going green.	**Key Words** Study vocabulary, and play a matching word game.
Pages 26-27 Test your knowledge of the greenest cities in the world.	**Pages 14-15** Find out more about green communities.	**Pages 20-21** View a video about green design.	**Slide Show** View images and captions, and try a writing activity.
Page 30 Complete the activity in the book, and then try creating your own debate.	**Pages 28-29** Learn more about green careers.		**AV² Quiz** Take this quiz to test your knowledge

Due to the dynamic nature of the Internet, some of the URLs and activities provided as part of AV² by Weigl may have changed or ceased to exist. AV² by Weigl accepts no responsibility for any such changes. All media enhanced books are regularly monitored to update addresses and sites in a timely manner. Contact AV² by Weigl at 1-866-649-3445 or av2books@weigl.com with any questions, comments, or feedback.